REJOIN the Brook just before the BURGHFIELD ROAD bridge: cross the road carefully & follow the left bank, past the allotments bridge, until you meet a track running under the railway.

IF the weather has be[en] under the bridge, foll[ow] & return under the ne[xt] go left to the end of [...] & right to the bridge.

MILL LANE

Hawkesbury Drive

Southcote Linear Park

Two Tier Bridge

Southcote Lock

Holybrook Farm

Burghfield Road

Milkmaid's Bridge

Burghfield Lock

Burghfield Mill

Clayhill Brook

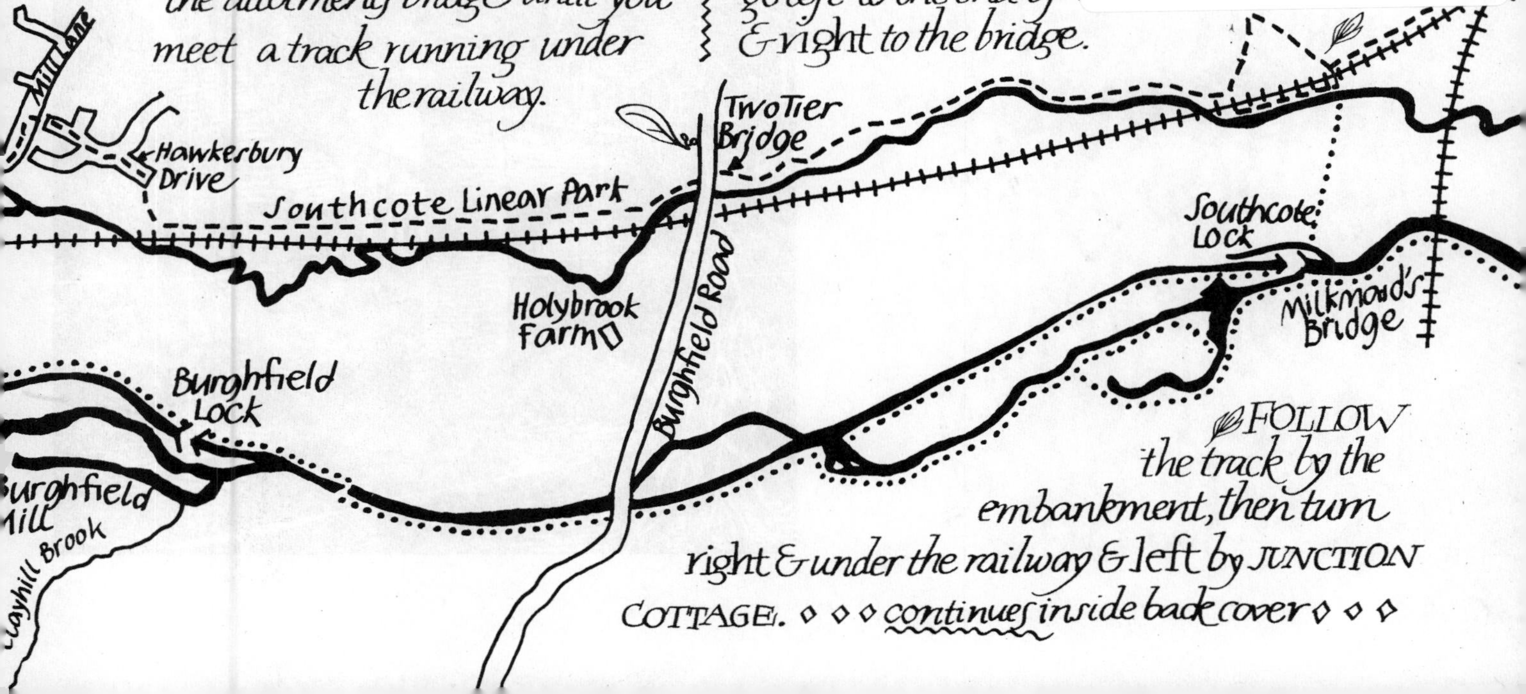

FOLLOW the track by the embankment, then turn right & under the railway & left by JUNCTION COTTAGE. ◇ ◇ ◇ continues inside back cover ◇ ◇ ◇

This UNIQUE and SECRETIVE WATERWAY has been HURRYING through and under READING for many CENTURIES

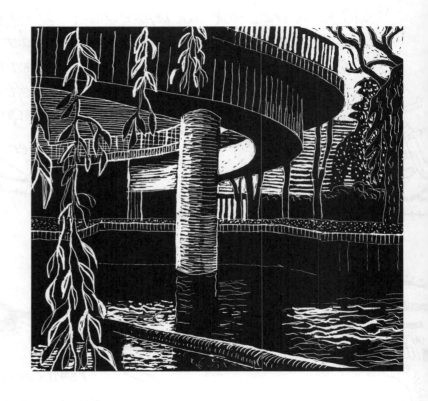

THE GRANATOR'S TALE

READING is lucky to have its two rivers, the Thames and the Kennet; both are navigable, and one of them is positively canalized. No-one, to my knowledge, has dubbed it The Venice of South Central England (though the Oracle's Riverside does regularly flood in imitation of the Piazza San Marco). Nevertheless, every June the Council stages an event called Waterfest, during which an enterprising boatman runs public trips around the town centre; and some of his passengers are surprised to find that you can indeed travel a circular route afloat.

THOSE who like to pore over old maps and accounts of the town will find that there was once a dense network of channels in the centre. Many have been filled in or diverted, but the Holy Brook remains, albeit secretively: its last half-mile might well be dubbed 'Holey' as it dives into a series of culverts, explorable only by the wetter sort of troglodyte. Every day thousands of people cross it unknowingly as they pass through Jackson's Corner; it is conspicuous under the Central Library, just visible beneath King's Walk, and newly revealed beside the Oracle. Many of the older generation can still remember it grinding corn at Soundy's (formerly the Abbey) Mill. But follow it upstream, afoot or on a map, and you will find that it is six miles long and clearly no ordinary, single-purpose millstream.

THE local historian Ernest Dormer, writing in 1937, argued that 'the Brook is more closely connected with the rise and progress of ancient Reading than the Kennet, and certainly the Thames'. Although for much of its life it defines the southern edge of the western suburbs, it does indeed pass nearer than either of the regular rivers to both of the spots that have been regarded at various times as the town's centre – the Butts and the Market Place – not to mention the demolished Yield Hall and (probably) the long-lost Castle. Dormer's account of the Brook (see Bibliography) is the fullest I have found; he was followed, more than half a century later, by Gordon

Spring, who – as an engineer working for the Borough Surveyor – had the benefit of inside (and underground) information. The third important published text is Hawkes and Fasham's archaeological report.

THE Brook ends peacefully at (Horse) Chestnut Walk, under the flinty chunks that are all we have of the mighty Reading Abbey; and a few yards upstream it undoubtedly drove their mill until as late as 1959. Its current name leads people to reasonably assume that it was created by – or for – the monks, some time after Henry Beauclerc set up the Benedictine establishment in 1121 AD; but a popular guidebook to the ruins suggests that it might be a wholly natural stream. Both Dormer and Spring realised that its upper reaches served at least one of the 5,624 mills mentioned in Domesday Book (1086), and that much of it therefore existed before the Abbey. Both writers agree with the early 19th century historian John Man's assertion that the monks' contribution was limited to extending it in the town centre; they certainly did not need to dig a six-mile leat to obtain water for any purpose. (There is an oft-copied story that their drinking supply came from Whitley Conduit (at Highgrove Street) in a pipe that tunnelled under the Kennet: this tale is supported by very little archaeological evidence, and Hawkes and Fasham agree with Spring that it seems unlikely. There was, after all, a well in the cloister.)

DORMER, who did not have the benefit of Gelling's research into place-names, wondered what the Brook was called before the monks arrived. This remains a mystery – perhaps various lengths had workaday names indicating their local function – but we do know that the first surviving mention of a Holy name – in the form 'Halowid Brook' – is not found until after the Dissolution, in the Itinerary of John Leland. The earliest name we have, in a 14th century annotation referred to below, is 'Garenter's Brook'; Gelling quotes a document of 1441 referring to 'Graniteresbrok', and (crucially) another of 1552 helpfully mentioning 'Le Granator's Broke als [also] le Hallowed Broke'. A modern map of the town centre, based on a 1552 description, shows the stream as 'Granalock alias Holy Brook'. A granator, garenter or granger was the owner or master of a grange or granary; the Abbey, indeed, had an office called the Granetary. The connexion with milling is obvious.

[4]

THE change to holiness seems to have been adopted rapidly; was it a pious reaction to the events of 1539? By 1560, Elizabeth I's charter for Reading uses 'Hallowed' and 'Hollowed' on the same page; other variants were plain 'Hollow' (a reasonable name for the culverted bits) and 'Holly' (quite misleading, as Ilex Aquifolium is by no means a waterside tree). The matter of nomenclature is further confused by four or five probable red herrings. In 1241 there is a single local mention of one Robert de Hollebroc, but it seems unlikely that our Brook would have become a surname so soon. An item in the Abbey Cartularies (a catalogue of its deeds and documents) refers to a Holiwater Lane in 1307, but this seems to have been a turning off what is now Friar Street, and at this date the word always meant the stuff you sprinkle. Large churches often generated religious street-names, such as Amen Court and Paternoster Square near St Paul's Cathedral. A 1920s newspaper article claimed Holy Water Lane as a precursor of Duke Street (which is supposed to be for the Duke of Somerset, who won some Abbey land) as it led from the south gate to the Brook. An account of Reading by Amyce in 1552 nicely compounded things by referring to 'Gruntersbroke'. And in 1650 a survey of ex-Abbey property referred to a fishable stream called 'Graunte's Brook alias Gunter's Brook'. Which water was meant? The present Gunter's was a much shorter, smaller millstream on the other side of the Kennet.

Brooks, however artificial, must run downhill: this one loses a total of about 25 feet, including a solitary sheer drop at Calcot Mill – at an average gradient of about 1 in 1300. (This is roughly the same as the Great Western main line through Reading, known as 'Brunel's Billiard Table'.) The modern Brook-walker has a choice of direction. Going with the flow, from bifurcation to re-confluence, seems 'natural', and romantics will sympathise with the water as it leaves Country to tangle with Town; those weary of Urbs, however, can enjoy a sense of escape as they go upstream in search of Rus – which they will encounter surprisingly soon. The following description takes the former course; I have tried, while telling of what you will see today, to incorporate what I have discovered of its history.

The first problem is to define its beginning and end. Just south of Theale, near Sulhamstead Lock, there is a narrow offshoot of the Kennet known (self-explanatorily) as 'Draper's Osier Bed Stream'. The Ordnance Survey's six-inch sheet of 1881 curiously chose to label this isolated watercourse 'Holy Brook', but all other maps and authorities agree that it starts lower down at a spot called Arrowhead. At the other end, Fred Thacker surprisingly asserted in 1932 that the Brook runs on from Chestnut Walk through Huntley and Palmers to Blake's Lock, failing to realise that this much bigger water is the natural, crooked, pre-canal Kennet.

The valley between Newbury and Reading is wide and flat, and the river may well have split and shifted of its own accord before man started messing about with it. The multiple watercourses one sees on the map now are a mixture of natural streams and man-made channels dug for assorted purposes: irrigation, drainage, power, drinking, washing and transport. Sheffield and Garston Locks mark the start and finish of one of the many navigation cuts made in 1724 to allow boats to reach

Newbury, and the Holy Brook (as now defined) leaves the residual main river between these two points at Arrowhead. It then follows fairly closely the southern edge of the Chiltern chalk, collecting water from whatever permanent or seasonal streams may run off the slopes.

To quote Leland again: 'The Arme that breketh out of Kenet is caullid the halowid Brooke, and brekith out of the principal streame of Kenet up above the Toune by West South West aboute the Bere, where thabbat of Reading had a fair Manor Place of Bryke...'. The Abbot's summer residence, built or acquired about 1232, was at Bere Court above Pangbourne; as Dormer pointed out, this is three miles from Arrowhead. Leland's 'aboute' is vague, and he may just have tossed together two

[8]

things he had learnt about the Abbey. He does not seem to have gone to look for himself: he arrived on his whistle-stop tour from Twyford and left via Caversham towards Henley. A deposition of 1596 says, more precisely, that the Brook 'taketh Hedde at the lower end of a mead called the theale Mead...'. This sounds like Arrowhead all right, but it goes on to say 'it had been dyverted out of the said river at the wear not far from Sowthcote Howse at Hadsey Ditche'. This apparent double source is explained below.

ARROWHEAD is not publicly accessible, even from Arrowhead Road. There is no weir, merely a V-shaped divider which now diverts about two-fifths of the Kennet's flow into the Brook. Spring tells us that it was renewed in 1890 (at a cost of £2500); the fraction was formerly a third, and the 1596 document says a half. At this point both the Brook and the residual Kennet are more wiggly than they would need to be if they were mere millstreams for Calcot and Burghfield respectively, so both are almost certainly natural branches. As Dormer says '...perhaps the word serpentine is not sufficiently indicative, for no serpent could by any

contortion form the sinuosities of this waterway in parts of its course.' And as far as the railway bridge (the first of four in three kilometres) the Brook follows a long-standing administrative boundary: there are many instances of bounds following the ancient courses of rivers, so I suggest that this initial stretch was once the larger part of the Kennet.

IF you have approached from Theale by the Navigation towpath you will have noticed, beside the turf-sided Garston Lock, two concrete pillboxes which formed part of an elaborate network set up by General Headquarters in 1940 to halt a German invasion. They are larger than usual because they mark a strategically significant point: the junction of the Green Stop Line, which followed the canal, and the Red, which came down the Thames and through the Sulham Gap. You will also have used the first level crossing of any kind on the main line out of Paddington. If you started from the bus stop on Charrington Road, however, you have come through the Holy Brook Linear Park, passing the Beansheaf Community Centre. This houses the Holybrook Parish Council, who publish an eponymous newsletter.

BETWEEN the two railway bridges the boundary wanders off to the south of the line, and the Brook enters what is almost certainly its first artificial cut as the millstream for Calcot. On this first walkable reach you are already in a public park with appropriate furniture, but it doesn't feel entirely tamed. Here are some exceptionally tall alder trees; they positively enjoy having wet feet. A sluice normally takes some of the flow back to the Kennet just before Calcot Mill, which operated as late as 1966, when a fire put an end to its working life – and hence to the Brook's primary purpose. The Victorian painter John Singer Sargent stayed here awhile; his 'A Morning Walk' is thought to depict his sister standing by the Brook. Next to the restored mill stands a stripey house called, appropriately, The Granary; its garden is the Brook's prettiest moment. There was a boathouse here in 1899 (as there was downstream at Coley Park Farm) but any navigation would probably have been strictly for pleasure. There are sarsen stones outside Holybrook Cottage by the bend in Mill Lane, and – further up – a fine brick wall which will delight bond-fanciers.

THE Abbey is yet far off, but its influence is already felt in this part of the valley: they acquired much property in this area, including the Manors of Tilehurst (including Calcot) and Burghfield. They also owned Calcot Mill and (from 1240) a half share in Burghfield Mill. One Matthew de Burghfield had built a bridge 'across the water of Reading Abbey in Burghfield' according to a document of 1280; his grandson Peter was the Abbey's tenant when an intriguing deed was drawn up by three parties, sometime between 1270 and 1298. It says that 'the watercourse in Burghfield' shall in perpetuity run from the main stream of the Kennet through the middle of the eastern part of Peter's meadow called Chalnemeade as far as Dynbroke; it shall be ten feet wide at its entry and eight throughout its length; if it shall be impeded in any way, the abbot and convent and their successors may enter it, flood and repair it at their will. Peter's reward was a white monk's loaf from the Abbey's granger every Annunciation. Fishing rights were granted to one John de la Wik, in exchange for the Dynbroke which had become blocked. The tripartite agreement was annotated by a later monk (in a 14th century hand) identifying 'the watercourse' as the 'Garenter's Brook'. This is all very tantalizing: we do not know where Chalnemeade or Dynbroke were, but it does seem that the waters mentioned may have been part of our Brook.

THE Brook, as a milltail, re-passes under the railway, rejoins the European constituency boundary, and is probably again the real, winding Kennet – or a branch of it – as far as Holybrook Farm. Walkers must make do with Southcote Linear Park, north of the line; the Brook was re-aligned here to obviate the need to build yet more bridges. Here you encounter two mysterious grassy-banked rectangles: they store excess surface-water from the surrounding roads, and in winter become makeshift ice-rinks. Regular Brook-followers suffer mild claustrophobia and withdrawal symptoms here, longing to trespass the forbidden bends beyond the tracks. This under-used green corridor – a planner's token barrier between suburb and railway – rather falls between stools, being neither field nor park. There are three alien-looking squares of grated bark furnished with playground equipment: two are built of steel in jarring primary colours, but the middle one is a more

sympathetic construction in wood. In the opener stretches there are already glimpses of Christchurch spire beckoning from its hilltop beyond Whitley Pump. Out of sight away to your left is the Holybrook Centre, with a scruffy car park called Holy Mead. By now you can probably no longer hear the swish of the M4, but the quiet is regularly interrupted by the purr of Thames Turbos, the whine of HSTs, or the throaty roar of goods locomotives hauling Yeoman's ballast trains up from Somerset.

THE Burghfield Road crosses the Brook on an odd bridge, with one arch on top of another; it was evidently heightened in 1847, when the adjacent Hungerford branch railway was built. In 1979 somebody suggested that a 'towpath' might be taken across the lower deck, to avoid crossing the busy road – still a good idea. It is said that there was once a separate arch to one side for pedestrians, but that it was blocked up by Italian prisoners-of-war in WWII. If this was the case, the evidence has been obscured by the brickwork shoring up the embankments – which itself, however, looks pre-war. The POWs are also supposed to have straightened some

sections of the Brook in an attempt to confuse German pilots, but this is not corroborated by a comparison of old and new maps. How do these stories start?

Mute swans will be seen in these opener sections, but not many: each pair needs a certain area of water for their territory, and because the Brook is narrow they command a correspondingly longer stretch. In summer the banks are alive with the scratchy songs of nesting birds: the sedge warbler, the less-common reed warbler, and the whitethroat, which seems always to arrive on April 22. Like the sedge warbler, it sings while giving a peculiar display flight. In May you might well hear nightingales; their song often goes unrecognised, as they sing by day along with everybody else. A rare winter sighting might be the water rail, perhaps resorting to the Brook when the flooded gravel-pits – their preferred habitat – freeze over. The little grebe or dabchick will dive if you see it, reappearing somewhere else up to 25 seconds later. Sparrowhawks have been known to build their substantial nests in Brook-side trees.

A more pleasing and less formal green belt follows the double bridge. Here you can find the spindle tree, with one of nature's more bizarre colour-schemes: its bright pink fruits open to reveal startling orange seeds. Holy Brook School stands a little to the north. Organized leisure is still on the agenda, with discreet fishing platforms: the Evening Post's angling correspondent assures us that 'South Reading's stretch of the Holy Brook is one of those rare waters that fishes better in the winter than the summer'. Children of all ages will be tempted to climb the great willow that grows aslant. Along the far bank are some quiet allotments, guarded by a scarecrow wearing a hi-vis lime-green police jacket. Back gardens come very close beyond the access bridge, but this is one of the nicest reaches, secretive and overhung. Across the water, stands of French-style riverside poplars are full of birdsong. A leat branched off here to serve Southcote Manor (built 1588, demolished 1921) and fill its moat – which is still to be seen, drily defending a banal block of flats off Hatford Road.

WHEN the Brook again parts company with rights of

way, the walker finds himself in fields where people used to set aside their old cars and furniture; happily the Council has put a stop to this practice. Thacker, arriving down Circuit Lane in 1909, wrote: 'the Holy Brook swirled fresh and clear the November day I saw it; and looking down from the little bridge you may discern how all the level land leans gently down to Kennet a meadow or two beyond.' The levelness is more apparent than the lean.

FROM Southcote Junction you are on the old Great Western branch-line: it makes a fine walk in its own right, rich with hips, haws, blackberries and feral strawberries, like an old Nature Study poster. Six furlongs and four chains long, it was opened as late as 1908 to serve Esso Oil, the Co-op jam factory, Baynes's timber-yard and the Fobney Street maltings; it closed in 1983. The only legal passengers it ever carried were railway enthusiasts on special trains: one ran on 3 October 1957, another on 5 February 1967. At first you are in a cutting, its soft sides colonised by foxes; but soon you are following a highish embankment. The path is narrow but purposeful: you can't see far ahead, but it's obviously going somewhere. The fields either side have the remains of lateral ridges which were part of an elaborate but low-maintenance water management system; at present the Brook is allowed to breach its banks and flood when necessary, creating a Mesopotamian, between-two-seas effect. To the north you overlook an area of unmanaged reedbed, where roe deer can sometimes be spotted. The other 'wild' animal of any size you might see is the American mink, which looks like a small, dark-brown-to-black otter. Having escaped (or been released) from farms, they have formed successful feral populations, but their numbers seem to fluctuate considerably – perhaps they move on when they've gobbled up all the water voles. These in turn are now scarce, but you may hear one plop into the water at your approach.

THIS whole stretch, and particularly the forbidden bit we have bypassed, is dominated by a set of stately plane trees, no doubt planted by an owner of Coley Park House; they are popular with crows, rooks and especially jackdaws, who prematurely blacken the sky as they come in their thousands to roost here at dusk. One

magnificently isolated tree shades a bend of the Brook, marking the best spot for a picnic. Just beyond lies Heron Island, which once had some of Reading's tallest birds' nests; reflected in the water are Reading's tallest flats at Coley Park. Herons are still to be seen, though they now live elsewhere; the island still has a fine specimen of the rare Black Poplar. To your left there is a good glimpse of the big house, which tapped the Brook to fill its ornamental lake. The left bank at this point is a little-known park called Coley Holybrook Walk. At The Brookmill there is a bit of a class barrier: in 2001 the occupants of this executive enclave erected an 'elephant fence' barring access to Coley allotments, but this has happily been removed. Here are a listed dovecote, barn conversions, pseudo-barn conversions, and a good deal of architectural fantasy trying to be another Portmeirion. The name 'Brookmill' is modern; Kenneth Major, in his piece on Berkshire watermills (BAJ, 1963) lists this as the site of 'a small farm mill'. A 1977 study of what might be done to improve Reading's waterways suggested that this spot – now an important footpath junction – would be a good site for a pub. Here are two low-arched bridges, both Listed Structures; Dormer tells of a member of the

Vachell family killing a monk for the crime of carrying hay over one of them, still known as Monks' Bridge. Just beyond here the archaeologists found, in the 1980s, a single stake of birchwood, radiocarbon-dated to 655-760 AD. It was interpreted as a channel marker rather than part of a revetment or 'an attempt at formal control'. This is a welcome piece of evidence apparently confirming the existence of a pre-Domesday Brook at this point.

To the south stands another Black Poplar, and in the middle of the field a particularly large and venerable Crack Willow. This untidiest member of the vegetable kingdom is the Brook's characteristic tree: its alternative English name, Brittle Willow, translates the scientific one, Salix Fragilis. Its breakability is actually a clever survival technique: the twigs and small branches that crack or snap off so easily will readily root to grow clones of the original tree, forming (as here) an ever-widening circle, like fairy-ring mushrooms on a lawn. Where, more usually, they stand by running water, the bits are carried downstream, lodge in some bankside obstruction, and again take root. They are often pollarded.

The scene on the right bank is still amazingly rural, though the Civic Centre is now less than a mile away. Here the Brook decides to go straight for once, and is conspicuously embanked, making it hard to believe that this bit is 'natural'. This is the only stretch that sees any kind of regular navigation: the odd numbers in Trelleck Road have dinghies at the bottoms of their gardens. You can't paddle far, but it must be pleasant to float along under the willows on a hot day. Yellow flag, hemlock and ladies' smock are still about, along with the flowering rush: this is hard to spot for most of the year, mingling with tall grasses, but in midsummer it bursts into clusters of pinky-white flowers. There is also a short row of Lavateras or tree-mallows, presumably escaped from across the water; in these globally-warmed days they can flower into December. From here on, Weeping Willows predominate over Crack. The field on your right was used, in 1883, as the Reading Volunteer Rifle Range. Old Coleyites remember this bit as being 'sparkling and clean; one could always see the gravel bottom and shoals of minnows and dace'. The north bank skirts the site of several brickworks and the associated chalk mine that

caused so much trouble at Field Road. Holybrook Road is the other side of Coley Rec; like most places that have borrowed the name, it is out of sight of the Brook itself.

A large retail shed marks the final transition from country to town, as the narrow gap (which has been dubbed 'Coley Gorge') crowds together Brook, Kennet, main road and dead railway. In 1985 the archaeologists dug around Rose Kiln Lane, finding an artificial bank four metres north of the present Brook. They saw this as 'a post-mediaeval towpath', but the report as a whole does not suggest a navigational use, or indeed commit itself as to how much of it is natural and how much artificial. Despite the cramping, here begins official amenitization: Reading Borough Council has provided a set of handsome, but so far under-used, laminated footbridges. On the right you will hear, before you see it, Reading's own Niagara, a wide weir over which much of the flow returns to the Kennet. Was this the site of an early mill? A notice appears to prohibit the playing of ball games (water polo?) in the Brook. In 1911 a draw-off on the left filled Coley's outdoor swimming bath: Spring says that it was popular with early morning bathers, who 'thought they bathed in fresh running water'. When the GWR built the Coley branch they had to make a culvert at least eighteen inches in diameter to take floodwater back to the Kennet.

COMMERCIAL pressure, measured in pounds per square foot, now leaves the Brook only the narrowest of green corridors behind the flats of Laud Close. Its banks are fenced off for their own protection, but this doesn't stop people from indulging the urge to throw things into any body of water: it just makes it harder to remove the rubbish. We are now into shopping trolley territory; these and other detritus may, however, provide nesting sites for coots. The smaller, shyer moorhen prefers to live out of sight in deep cover. Bird life is otherwise restricted now, though you may still be lucky enough to see the kingfisher's blue flash. They nest in all sorts of holes: decayed trees, drainpipes, gun emplacements.

BEYOND Berkeley Avenue – itself graced with an avenue of planes – you are in one of the less modernized corners of Old Coley, with some good examples of Reading patterned brickwork. Brook Street West is the

last remaining riparian terrace; plain Brook Street, which presumably came first, used to mirror it across the stream but gave way to the railway and later to the big bad A33. Willow Street used to cross hereabouts. The Brook played a large part in the life of this urban village. It is claimed that wild watercress was gathered somewhere on this stretch (it can still be found further upstream); that in the absence of domestic baths people would take a dip in it for a good clean-up; children regarded it as 'a proper little lido'; and we hear of a policeman being thrown into the water, either for daring to intervene in a domestic fight outside the Blue Lion or for boasting that he would 'clean up' Coley single-handed. Both versions of the story agree that he bore no grudge the next day.

THE Brook slides under the concrete road-raft, and willows still shade the scene where it emerges by the Sally Army hostel, while a boom collects waterborne rubbish and provides a literal rat-run. At the top of Castle Street stands Holybrook House, a fine 18th century dwelling; F M Underhill, writing in the Reading Mercury in 1969, wondered whether the grotesque head over its door was intended to represent 'the spirit of the Holy Brook'. (The name Holybrook House has since been borrowed for some new flats off Fobney Street.) In the Maltings estate, with its water-friendly street-names, the Brook begins to play hide-and-seek. At the foot of the Vachel almshouses a sluiced channel heads off south to rejoin the Kennet just below the weir of County Lock: the whole Brook can be diverted down here for culvert inspections or building operations. In 1876 there were glasshouses over the next short section of the Brook. Spring passes on what sounds like an urban myth about a lady giving birth as she fell into the water from a lavatory at the bottom of a garden in Castle Street: one in, two out. (This looks like a version of the Duke Street story recounted below.) More plausible are Phoebe Cusden's tales of people bathing and fishing along here – and even swimming along to visit their neighbours. The Brook gets very hedged and overgrown along Mallard Row, and finally goes to ground behind Maltings Place; beside Plaza West you can see running water beneath a circular grating. The culvert along here is another Listed Structure; it was investigated by archaeologists in the 1980s, and a detailed description is to be found in Hawkes

and Fasham. Most of it was brick-built, probably in the 18th and 19th centuries, but 22 metres were covered with 12th and 13th century stonework, some of it carved; this was undoubtedly liberated from the ruined Abbey and assembled here soon after the Dissolution. Another 11 metres had a ribbed arched roof. It is, in 2003, sagging and in need of repair.

THE Brook passes under Bridge Street where the northernmost of the Seven Bridges would have been (this name is found in documents as early as 1285, though no old map shows quite so many). It can be seen again through a fence on your left; this derelict patch could do with some gardening. A number of premises along Gun

Street extend over the Brook; in the 1920s Messrs E Poynder & Son traded as The Holybrook Press from nos. 3–4. A lot of money has been spent on landscaping where it skirts the Oracle, its most populous spot: steps, a footbridge with a beautiful maple-leafy glass roof, railings, seats and a reedmacy sculpture. But the sun rarely penetrates this canyon, and the Brook hurries through with waving waterweed, its ferny walls pierced by mysterious holes and archways. The shopping centre has put up several information boards about the Kennet, but not its little sibling; a nod of recognition is to be found in the naming of the Holy Brook Walk (aka the Lower Mall) and Car Park. On this site, after the old brewery had been demolished, the brick vault of the next culverted section was exposed to view while Oxford Archaeology excavated the 1628 Oracle workhouse.

THEY concluded from geological deposits that the Brook was, at this point, a natural stream. There was evidence of chalk quarrying on these slopes, probably from Saxon times, and of flimsy timber-framed structures – probably houses – from c1075. In the first decades of the 12th century, a very well-constructed stone house with a large central hearth was built, probably for a merchant, on the north bank of the Brook. In about 1267 this was extended and probably linked by a bridge to a new building on the south bank. These premises may have been used for dyeing or some other industrial purpose that used the Brook's water. The site was probably later occupied by a tannery, where animal hides were soaked in water mixed with urine and dogs' faeces. One regrettable loss to the shopping mall was an elegant bridge with four-centred arches, the oldest in Reading. This carried a lane which formed part of a grid of streets – possibly planned and imposed by the Abbey – superimposed on a grid of watercourses which served various human purposes in addition to controlling floods.

HAWKES and Fasham also give some attention to the intricacies of the various streams in the town centre (Grey's Lock Stream, Simonds' Ditch, Maltmyll Broke, Plat Brook etc). St Giles's and Minster Mill Streams explain themselves; the latter has always been a parish boundary, and this again suggests that it may be a natural branch adapted by man. Spring was convinced that the Brook and other streams were used for transport, but this seems unlikely. The mills would have obstructed traffic, the Kennet is always very close, and although several 'locks' are named on waters other than the main river, the word did not always imply the boat-chamber we mean today; Tan Lock and Girdwick's Lock are listed as 'fisheries' at the Dissolution.

GORDON Spring had to inspect these subterranean lengths once a year. He had the Brook drained at Castle Street and donned waders, but there were still 'wet holes of uncomfortable depth'. He could tell where he was by the nature of the detritus: crockery and cutlery under the Ship Hotel, tools from an ironmonger's, and a great pile of beer bottles by Simonds' brewery. Other adventurers have canoed through; see Hall and Coleclough. In King's Walk, running water is just visible under a circle of barely translucent glass; around it runs the message 'Listen closely to the Holy Brook, for through it flows time itself'. After a couple of seconds' contemplation this doesn't seem terribly profound – and if the adjacent 'water feature' is working you can't hear it anyway. Through the window you can see the Brook diving under the Ship. Nearby stood the old Yield Hall, where town

business was conducted until 1543; a move to a new Town Hall at Greyfriars was prompted by complaints that 'the river' (not necessarily the Brook) was 'the common washing place of the most part of the town... there is such a beating of battledores (or washing beetles) as one man cannot hear another...'.

A more comprehensive picture of the town-centre Brook, its functions and its condition survives from 1575, when Orders, Acts and Decrees were made by 'Commissioners appointed under a Commission of Sewers'. Townspeople were said to 'have chiefly their water to brew, bake and dress their meat' out of it. It was to be deepened and cleansed, and its banks were to be repaired and encroachments removed; builders were to remove 'tiles, mortar or other stuff'; any person having a gutter running into it was to make a grating, the bars of which should not be 'above half an inch asunder', so that nothing but water may pass; the Corporation was to make 'grass hatches' (evidently some sort of grating) to prevent the washing of gravel and soil into it; hogsties and stables were not to drain into it; horses were not to be watered or washed in it; no person was to throw into it any horns, bones, sheep's feet, dust, straw, rushes, dirt, weeds, gravel, ashes, ridding of lime pits, tan vats, etc, or suffer any buck [washing] water or other filthy water to run into it. The occupier of the Abbey Mill was to make a monthly inspection for nuisances. Again, in 1594: 'No person or persons shall from henceforth put or convey any kind of dyeing liquor or woad liquor into or upon any part of the street or common soil of this borough, or into the Hallowed Brook.' On Christmas Eve, 1628, four men were accused of 'laying their soil at the grates by the Hallowed Brook'. Professional scavengers were employed to clean these grates or gratings: one Richard Absolon was paid twenty shillings a year to do so in 1662.

IT seems probable that apart from its main industrial functions the Brook was maintained for centuries as a provider of clean water. London opened its 38-mile New River to bring a drinkable supply from Hertfordshire in 1613. Reading perhaps already enjoyed such a source, and it would be nice to be able to prove that it was consistently healthier than comparable towns from the 12th to the 17th centuries because of the Holy Brook. In 1641 the Corporation's Diary notes a proposal for some

sort of piped supply; its promoters wanted to see a plan
of the New River scheme (on which, indeed, Reading's
own John Blagrave had worked as a surveyor). A water
company was eventually set up in 1696, but its pumps
were inadequate and its wooden pipes didn't reach many
houses; the next serious attempt to improve the supply
was in 1820, when the Mill Lane tower was built and
Cubitt put his Tank up at Whitley. Both of these
enterprises drew from the Kennet near Bridge Street, but
it is likely that the people of Coley – probably not
connected to the early piped system – continued to use
the Brook. In the mid-19th century, as the population
rose alarmingly and Public Health became a major
concern, it was proposed to use the Brook again;
Surveying Officers reported in 1851 that it was 'in its
ordinary condition salubrious and well suited for
domestic purposes'. In the event they moved the intake
out to Southcote, still on the Kennet.

COMING to the Duke Street/King's Road junction, we
find in the Abbey Cartulary several items which may well
refer to the Brook at this point, without giving it a name
(or even calling it a millstream). Before 1186 we read of

land 'between the Kennet and the new ditch' (fossa); between that date and 1300 there are mentions of 'the two courses of the Kennet', 'the two watercourses', 'the larger and smaller waters of the Kennet'; and in 1348 'land on High Street between the two bridges'. If the Brook was already running through the Oracle site in 1121, the monks had only to dig a very short 'new ditch' for their mill. The earliest surviving map of Reading is John Speed's of 1610, by which time High Street/Duke Street crossed the Brook, the Kennet and the later, diminutive Gunter's Brook. Leaping forward to 1878, we have the Reading Tramways Order stipulating that the bottom of the sleepers or other foundation for the rails of the new system must be at least four inches above the stonework or brickwork of the Brook's culverts.

IN The Land of the Gap (1937) J H Baker relates another lady-falling-in story, dating from perhaps the 1860s: she was a tobacconist, and her Duke Street shop had a dodgy floor. One fine day it duly gave way; but her capacious crinolines bore her up, and she emerged unscathed at Abbey Mill. Cecilia Millsom's Tales of Old Berkshire

(1977) gives her a name – Mrs Ball (she does not, alas, appear in the old street directories) – and makes her pregnant, though this time the infant did not appear until she was on dry land; he was duly christened 'Holybrook'. His later 'chestiness' was attributed to his antenatal dip. Less fortunate was the poet Stephen Duck: born in 1705 to humble Wiltshire folk, he was taken up by the Court, though Alexander Pope didn't rate his verse. The powers-that-were made him a Yeoman of the Guard and ordained him priest, both apparently to give him a regular income. Some wag suggested he be appointed Keeper of Duck... He was employed for a while as a hermit in an artificial cave in the grounds of Queen Caroline's Richmond Lodge, which later became Kew Gardens. Eventually he went mad, and in 1756 'drowned himself in a fit of dejection in a trout stream behind the Black Lion at Reading'. This is assumed to have been our Brook. The next half-century saw many unintentional fatalities: Michael Hinton records that people alive in 1817 could recall 101 children falling into the unfenced Brook.

THE Corporation Terrier (list of Council properties) for 1908 reveals that in 1874 George Palmer granted the Sanitary Authority the right to build over and cover in the Brook at Abbey Square. They were obliged, however, to put in a manhole with an iron door to allow the tenant of the Abbey Mill to clean it out. This may be the opening noted by Hall and Coleclough under the floor of what is now the Casa café-bar. The 1:500 map of 1876 shows a public urinal approximately where the front door of the library stands now; by this date, one hopes, no-one was obliged to drink from the lower Brook or Kennet. In 1956 the culvert along here was in danger of collapsing; when it became clear that repairs were going to cost far more than the Council's estimates, the Brook was re-classified as a Class 1 road for funding purposes. Creative accounting is not new. The bit behind the Central Library, with its story-telling brick theatre on the Greek pattern and its sinister air vents, is familiar to all readers. The Abbey stables were along here on the north bank. The penultimate lap, overshadowed by the backsides of unlovely 1960s buildings, is daunting: an attempt was made in 1988 to prettify it with out-of-place-looking pampas grass and other shrubs, but opportunist buddleias are staging a takeover. Bridges were erected, but at one point there is a ridiculous mauvais pas in the form of a 20-inch step which will defeat the less agile. Rats and rubbish are too common. The 1979 report mentioned above has pretty line-drawings of mini-piazzas leading through to the Abbey, and a current scheme (2002) promises great improvements, retaining and repairing the re-jigged mediaeval arch of the Mill. Spring says that this part of the Brook was shifted a little to the south to make room for a building that didn't happen, but this is not apparent from the maps. The Abbey Mill itself was one of the first in England (1868) to convert from stones to rollers.

So we come to the quiet re-confluence in the shadow of the office block known as the Green Giant, and under the last of the Brook's 33 bridges. Leland tells us that the Brook 'cumming doune by medowes ynto Reading toun passith thorough a peace of thabbay cleansing the filth of it, and a little lower joinith againe with the great streame'. Hawkes and Fasham's report of the 1979-84 digs at Abbey Wharf goes into great detail about the shifting

course of both river and Brook at this point. They also identified an apparent flood relief channel bypassing the Mill, and suggest that it might have served some monastic fishponds – and even that the monks may have encouraged the disposal of sewage into the Brook to make it more nutritious for the fish.

To this spot attaches one last tale, this time definitely and happily fictional. The Berkshire Bell, a short-lived magazine of the 1880s, printed a very Victorian story of hopeless mediaeval passion between a monk at the Abbey and a nun in a mythical convent up at Coley. She drowns herself for love in the Brook, is carried downstream, and guess who happens to be moping by the reredorter as she floats into view... they are re-united in a watery grave, and the curious consequence was that someone decided the Brook should henceforth be called Holy.

Ernest Dormer began his 1937 piece portentously: 'It is the fate of many rivers to take their rise in almost idyllic surroundings and finish their course amid the clamour of industry; to start their leisurely flow between banks fringed by the rosy spikes of the loosestrife and to end their travail in a stream carrying the flotsam and jetsam of a mercantile age.' From the evidence available he is correct to call it a river – a natural braid of the Kennet. 'Idyllic' is still not too strong a word for some of the upper reaches; post-war suburbia has reached, but not yet breached, the Brook's boundary between dry ground and wet. It served many industries over the centuries, all now gone. Plastic beakers now float on a Brook so clear that you can see the garbage on the bottom; its only uses are as an amenity – horrible word – and a relief channel for the turbulent Kennet. As a walking route to the west it is much slower than its parent's towpath, but the Holy Brook – unpredictable, unsanitized, hole-and-corner thing that it is – has many rewards for the determined explorer.

WALKING THE BROOK

THE INCLUSION OF A PATH IN THE TEXT OR ON THE MAP
DOES NOT IMPLY A FORMAL RIGHT OF WAY

✳

PARTS OF THE ROUTE CAN BE OVERGROWN IN SUMMER AND
MUDDY OR UNDER WATER AT ANY TIME

✳

WATERPROOF FOOTWEAR IS RECOMMENDED.

✳

CIRCULAR WALKS CAN BE DONE BY USING TWO
FOOTPATH LINKS TO THE KENNET NAVIGATION TOWPATH:
FROM CIRCUIT LANE TO SOUTHCOTE LOCK
AND FROM THE BROOKMILL TO FOBNEY LOCK.

BY THE SAME AUTHOR
& ALSO PUBLISHED BY TWO RIVERS PRESS:

✳

A Much Maligned Town:
Opinions of Reading 1586–1997

✳

Abattoirs to Zinzan:
Reading streets and their names

BIBLIOGRAPHY

COLEY LOCAL HISTORY GROUP: Talking of Coley and More
Talking of Coley, 1990-1
CORPORATION OF READING: Diaries and Minutes
MIKE COX: The Last Water Vole?, circa 2001
PHOEBE E CUSDEN: Coley, portrait of an urban village, 1977
ERNEST J DORMER: The Stream called the Hallowed Brook at
Reading in the Berks Archaeological Journal, vol. 41, 1937)
MARGARET GELLING: The Place-names of Berkshire, 1976
PIP HALL AND JONATHAN COLECLOUGH: 20,000 Leagues under
Reading, in Catalyst 50, September 1991.
J W HAWKES AND P J FASHAM: Excavations on Reading
Waterfront Sites 1979-88, 1997
MICHAEL HINTON: A History of the Town of Reading, 1954
J B HURRY: Reading Abbey, 1901
B R KEMP (ED): Reading Abbey Cartularies, 1986
JOHN MAN: History of Reading, 1816
ORDNANCE SURVEY: MAPS, various dates
C F PRITCHARD (ED): Reading Charters, Acts and
Orders 1253-1913, 1913
GORDON SPRING: Casual Ramblings Concerning the Early
Waterways of Reading and For Those in Peril on the
Canal, circa 1992
FRED S THACKER: Kennet Country, 1932

...and yet to come: in 2004 OXFORD ARCHAEOLOGY will be
publishing their report on the excavations they carried out
on the Oracle site.

ACKNOWLEDGEMENTS

READING CIVIC SOCIETY, WITH THE AID OF GRANTS
FROM THE LOCAL HERITAGE INITIATIVE AND THE
ENVIRONMENT AGENCY, HAS SPONSORED THIS
PUBLICATION AS PART OF THEIR HOLY BROOK PROJECT
TO INCREASE PUBLIC AWARENESS OF, AND ENCOURAGE
ACCESS TO, THE BROOK. THE AUTHOR WOULD LIKE TO
THANK THE FOLLOWING FOR HELP OF VARIOUS KINDS:
ADRIAN LAWSON OF READING BOROUGH COUNCIL
BEN FORD AND OXFORD ARCHAEOLOGY
READING LOCAL STUDIES LIBRARY

✳

TEXT © ADAM SOWAN

✳

ILLUSTRATIONS © PETER HAY

✳

DESIGN & LETTERING SALLY CASTLE

✳

ISBN 1 901677 34 6
PUBLISHED IN THE UK 2003 BY TWO RIVERS PRESS
www.tworiverspress.com

✤

PRINTED BY CONSERVATREE PRINT & DESIGN
RG4 8AU
www.conservatree.co.uk

READING CIVIC SOCIETY

READING CIVIC SOCIETY, FOUNDED IN 1962,
AIMS TO STIMULATE PUBLIC INTEREST IN THE TOWN, TO
PROMOTE HIGH STANDARDS OF ARCHITECTURE AND
PLANNING, AND TO SECURE THE PRESERVATION, PROTECTION,
DEVELOPMENT AND IMPROVEMENT OF FEATURES
OF HISTORIC INTEREST.
IT PLAYED A LARGE PART IN THE CAMPAIGNS TO SAVE THE
TOWN HALL AND MANSION HOUSE. IT ALSO ORGANISES
OUTINGS TO OTHER TOWNS AND PLACES OF HISTORIC AND
ARCHITECTURAL INTEREST.
IF YOU WOULD LIKE TO JOIN, PLEASE CONTACT THE
MEMBERSHIP SECRETARY AT 69 BAKER STREET RG1 7XY.
www.readingcivicsociety.org.uk

THE LOCAL HERITAGE INITIATIVE IS A PARTNERSHIP
BETWEEN THE HERITAGE LOTTERY FUND, NATIONWIDE
BUILDING SOCIETY AND THE COUNTRYSIDE AGENCY.

Local Heritage *initiative*

ENVIRONMENT
AGENCY

Heritage
Lottery Fund

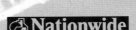

Nationwide

The
Countryside
Agency

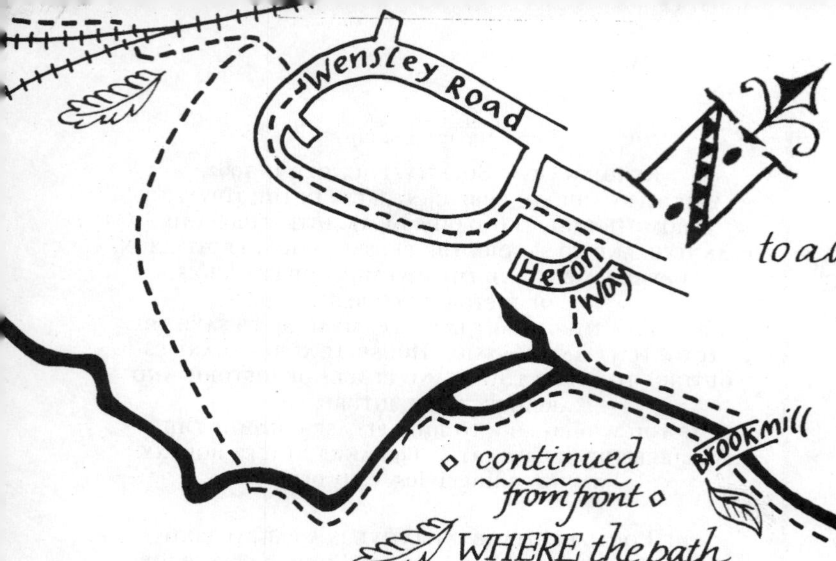

Wensley Road

Heron Way

Brookmill

FOLLOW the right bank to a wooden footbridge; cross it & turn right to ROSEKILN LANE; cross this & the road bridge & take a narrow path immediately on the left to rejoin the right bank. Cross the next footbridge & follow the left bank behind the flats to some steps up to BERKELEY AVENUE

◊ continued from front ◊

WHERE the path leaves the railway, turn right onto the old trackbed; where it crosses the Brook slide down on the left to join its right bank to the THE BROOKMILL. (If the mudslide is too daunting, or the Brook is flooding into the field, either continue to the A33 or return to the last junction, proceed by WENSLEY Rᴰ & HERON WAY to the COLEY HOLYBROOK WALK, & cross BROOKMILL bridge.)